Streaks of Light and the Subsequent Shadows

A Collection of Poetry

by

Jeffrey R. Erdman

Copyright © 2011 Brite Lite Publications

All rights reserved.

No part of this book may be reproduced or transmitted in any form or by any means, electronic or mechanical, including photocopying, recording, or by any information storage and retrieval system, without permission in writing from the publisher.

This collection is dedicated to all the people in my life who contributed to its creation, either directly or indirectly, through inspiration or otherwise.

But in particular to my Mother, *Diane,* and to my Father, *Ron* ~ For always believing in me, and always being there for me... No matter what. ~

Thanks to everyone who assisted in the creation of this collection, to my family, to my friends, and Everyone at *Journey to the Heart.*
Special thanks to *Ben Brush* for his brilliant work on the cover-art, and *Jason Sousa* for technical support.
Thanks especially to *Paul Benson*, who is a true inspiration. Without you, *Paul*, these words would not be in print.
Finally, I give a big thank you to everyone at Brite Lite Publications for all their hard work, and to those at createspace.com.

Note from the Poet:

These poems offer a glimpse into my life's experiences throughout the years 1999 – 2011. Many pieces are dated 2011 but actually stem from pieces written years earlier. At the bottom of each page I have included a short comment about the piece (space permitting). This was done to offer a little insight into what I was thinking or feeling when the piece was created. However, I will say that it is sometimes wiser to remain oblivious to original or intended sentiment. Oftentimes our own impressions are more important than the actual. Please note that all spelling and word choices, even the odd or incorrect, are intentional. I hope you can find pleasure in this look into one man's trail through life. May my many moods, perspectives and attitudes bring a smile to your face, a tear to your eye, and a beat to your heart. Enjoy!

Streaks of Light and the Subsequent Shadows
A Collection of Poetry
Jeffrey R. Erdman
ISBN-13: 978-0986866401
ISBN-10: 0986866407
BISAC: Poetry/Canadian

Brite Lite Publications
Nova Scotia, Canada
britelitepublications@gmail.com

Cover-art by Ben Brush
www.ben-brush.com

Contents

Streaks of Light and the Subsequent Shadows	1
Raindrops	2
Roses Are Red	3
Euphony	4
On the Rocks	5
Soliloquy	6
Mantra	7
Jetsam	8
Genesis	9
Intrinsic Inside	10
Deal?	11
Adrift	12
Reflection	13
Trust	14
Tricky	15
The Dawn of Dusk	16
Sunrise	17
Stars Crossed	18
Only One Girl	19
... And My Mind's Made Up	20
Captured	21
Possibly Pathetic	22
Reflex Reflects Choice	23
Backstroke	24
Vs.	25
Girl Talk	26
Kiss Me Kill Joy	27
In Bloom	28
Phantom Love	29
Pinch at Your Peril	30
Opposites React	31
A Party in 1999	32
A Friend In Me?	33
Pledge	34
The Worn Tracks of Yesterday	35
Emancipation Determination	36
After the War	37
Remedy	38
Next of Kin	39

Freehand	40
Star of Wonder	41
Hear Here	42
New Life Now	43
Somatose	44
Salvation	45
Lovely	46
Everessence	47
Elephant Shoe	48
Absence	49
Barking	50
Daily Dose	51
The Cracked Cocoon	52
Murdered Muse	53
Necrosis	54
Not Away Saga	55
Permission Radio	56
It's Genetic	57
My Spacey Place	58
Cradle My Child	59
The Modern Age	60
Sunny Tomorrow, With a Chance of Death	61
The Eagle	62
Fable	63
Mastercraft	64
Ego On Auto	65
Sun Kissed	66
Severance	67
In Perfect Focus	68
The Sweetness	69
Ray of Sunshine	70
Sick Ink	71
Expulsion	72
The Coronation of Reflection and Light	73
Unicorn	74
Fire Within	75
Story of My Life	76
Happily Ever After	77
The Devil's Fairy Tail	78
A Warm Place	79
In the Shade of a Bleeding Heart	80
Tomorrow	81

Streaks of Light

and the

Subsequent Shadows

Streaks of Light and the Subsequent Shadows

An epic choir of spectacular vernacular fills these ears with echo
It's the dawn's song descending from the towering spire of night
And the sunrise zephyr carrying a new promise of sweet salvation
Redemption climbs through the chronicles of this ancient cathedral
These heavenly halls full with the sweet verbose of the lovely life
And the light puts itself in the dew on every waiting spider's web

Lap up this blaring belched cacophony written in such common tongue
The cold sunrise slashes its colour across so many steel horizons
Another glorious morning that can only ravage the reckless in me
Daylight's redemption is but feeble charity for a shattered chrysalis
Clap a greedy slap grasp around this sun's throat and punish hard
Let misty manoeuvres ravish the Goddess when she presents her prize

Illustrate our illustrious illusions on this ill-fated day
Illuminate the luminous that alludes to the elusive
These are the streaks of light and the subsequent shadows
A collection of the sun, a collage of the fullest moons
Gather what the stars spill out from their distant lanterns
Find the finest streamer before it strangles your stranded heart

Every universe is but a grain of sand in this finger pinch
Humanity's but a crispy autumn leaf taunted by the wind
A raindrop supernova of the eternally omniscient ethereal
Crucial cradle to embracing grave, these are the lives of our days
Let this sunrise smear itself across the putrid filth accumulated in the core
These words are the light, and the shelter of shade that cools a summer's day

JRE
2011

The collection was named before this piece was conceived. I found myself overcome with impressions granted by the title and thought those impressions expressed might make an appropriate introduction to my work. The gist of this is that our world is made up of two different views, fundamentally either positive or negative. It's up to you to see the side you prefer and make that the sight you see with.

Raindrops

A sleek silk dream drifting along in my favourite fantasy stream
How it seems to have the theme of the sweetest life that has ever been
A saturated soul in a gasoline rainbow puddle that's leaked into the river
It's a purified demise as our soul flows back to the lost place it used to know
Soaking up the sacred memory as it passes by these treacherous turmoil times
Sailing senseless on a seeping slightly, slowly seeking stream of soft smile
Then gently from the sudden season come the songs of a magnificent morning
It's the trickling taste of the next life now that mingles with the redeeming dawn
Quick creamy currents crash in waves over the galvanized grip of the past
Dripping drops of yellow pink sunspots in the bubbling, foamy swells
A splashing laugh of baby birth spills and cascades over this soul-rise
Our long river ends just around the bend and is merely water to the trees
The white light dream of a feather on a breeze, and the rippling reminder of the rain

JRE
2009

Written to show the many and varied journeys we take through life, and how each path has its own unique beauty, if we only look a little deeper. Maybe this is trying to say that life is as random as the rain.

Roses Are Red

Sands of time flow through tiny holes in my life
As the piles grow I finally see how far I've wandered
Memory is surrounded by these travels
Encroached upon from all fronts
My sight covers the entire world in dust
I see now with my finest eye
Orchids clutter vanity's vision
My belligerent tromp will crush their jungle
I stumble and collapse into my final chance
A thicket of thorns is actually hope
Even as the pricks take their prize
I crawl the last miles of my life
That yummy elixir is all I find
And I drink down that sweet denial
Replenish this creature enough to plod on
Grasping for the red bloom that could never be a lie

JRE
2011

Reworked from a piece written in 2002, this is about my tendency to over look an orchid while searching for a rose.

Euphony

Your essence clings to me like a residual scent
A haunting torture for memory to endure
But I gladly hold that vivid reminiscence today
For all else will fade into forgotten
I fiddle with the lockets of love
The sun says this can be my task
To give my days to the trouble that has ever been
Sweetness gathers in our secrets
Music riding chariots of fire along the silver shore
Footprints in the sand of the oldest arena
A trumpet sets its twirling crescendo on the wind
As a voice calls from beyond the far side of the world
I solve the mystery of the fog soaked sea
And the sound comes forth like pregnant words
"Take this halo and wear it well"
Washed over and absorbed into fictitious fantasy
Pick just one dream from all these scenes
The one that says we are golden

JRE
2011

This piece was reworked since its initial conception in 2006. It's about finding the person who you are on the inside, the true you.

On the Rocks

Mesmerize my memory with sweet times you recall
Speak them through your skin to me so that I might taste it all
Captivate my core and feed it your happy thoughts
I relish in deliciousness, but it is my life that you've bought
My nonsense dream super scheme
My lonely tired voice
Chorus cough of crimson cream
All the reasons not yet seen
Polished packaged pretty lives
Beloved whores and forgotten wives
Needle-pricks to money-quicks
Always-sicks to never-sticks
Flaming faiths to folly-flops
Tantalized triggers to all tree chops
Choices chose chew till through
Bite till blood does flow from you
With fiction past remembered true
The love of all washes over new
Stay today to see this smile
A precious moment of human trial
Tell the tale of this life true
And all that is shall be owned by you

JRE
2008

Literally written while sitting on a pile of rocks, this work was accomplished in one take with only three real-time edits. I'd say this piece is a series of random observations about life.

Soliloquy

Milky Shadows on the sunlight sand
Mischievous melodies grasped in my hand
Sing the song of tomorrow's times
Tell me the words that always rhyme
My silver shell of frosty dust
Cancel scent perfume, foggy thick musk
Dawn of dread and rise of light
Sailing through dreams, the crimson kite
Happy horror promise, sublime lip kiss
Dangle drip mourning of fine reminisce
Smile for me and smile for you
Slip daydream doorway delivery due

JRE
2008

One day this poured out of me as is, just a gush of good mood that found form with pen and paper.

Mantra

Bumble blunder cast asunder
Mingle muddle mother wonder
Dreamy dose of daisy days
Pump the pleasant past away
Mutter love her traffic thunder
Viviparous vase of sister and brother
Quicksand chant of jungle juice
Tripping trance that has no use
Dip the memory in the now
Passion bubble burst allowed
Leaky latch of lover's luck
Swallow quickly double sucked
Insipid words that sound like taste
Precise expression gone to waste
Rival riddle on the silk full moon
Vertebrae tree spun on lilac loom
Lonely fable flying through mind
Tempt taint torture all the time

JRE
2008

Sometimes I have an immense urge to write but there are so many thoughts and feelings ready to burst out that it's difficult to find precision. This is the result.

Jetsam

Old hopes wash up on the beach of desire
The words from the past forgotten, repressed
Things are now put away. Away where time may keep them

Moments fade to years as all these things disappear
Yet dreams of the future seem renewed, refreshed
Time to dust off an echo? An echo of our sweetest silence

Illusions fill the void of this old drowned reality
But pain, now scars is soaked up, rung out
Hearts now set free. Free from the burdens of the circle

A whisper of love so softly in your ear
In lust for lost passions that ensnare, invoke
Senses seem to spin. Spin so wildly beyond control

New feeling moves to catch us and steady this faltered course
Now tomorrow finds us here in our hesitation, waiting
Love is all of our desire. Desire is the sea we are lost on

JRE
2003

One of my earliest coherent pieces, this is about friends getting tangled up in love.

Genesis

My path before me is my long walk of sorry
Sulking under the shadow branches that reach over me
Dark forest with water wet and toothless trees that don't forget
A demon screams from across the stream and shatters my desire dream
The sudden shudder creeping inside is the forsaken person who I did let die
Pace of passion quickens slowly, dragging him from the depth of my memory
My gilded guilt is a lonely burden that I manifest and let own me solely
Run red river blood that rinses the wretched that resides in me
Casting off the chaos of gripping grime that grinds my time
Leave me here as the lonely so that I might know thee
Here I shall rummage through and then reside
The living of this life in the expulsive mind
Try truth to see what is born of me
Revive a life that is not my crime
Spiral time to rise and shine

JRE
2008

This is a piece about starting over, or the reinvention of oneself. I remember writing this shortly after researching the song "Lateralus" by Tool. There's a hint of those personal impressions coming through.

Intrinsic Inside

Innocent eyes stare into me
They find me in dreams and ask
And every moment becomes an invitation
I'm lulled away by soft gravity's grip
The swift collapse into coalescence
Then bright shiny love showers down
And connection is made in the middle
Vacancy is conquered by a planted presence
A seed grows underneath my heart
My life is the sun that will shine
My body is the soil that will hold
Time forgets and gives itself away
Choices change into such sublime faith
We both wake up to the unbreakable bond
We both wake up to a new life

JRE
2011

This was spawned from a 2004 piece originally about a friend and her young son. It's become a piece about pregnancy in general, and the life changes involved. I wanted to put some of the sacredness back into something we've let become so sterile, so medical.

Deal?

Of all the things to look at
Of all the things to hold
Of all the love that is in this world
For yours my soul is sold

JRE
2004

Short, sweet, and self explanatory. This piece used to be the ending to another, but I prefer it when it stands on its own.

Adrift

My heart is a strange vessel
Setting its sails despite all this excess cargo
Voyages weighed down by burdens that need not be carried
Some may not understand why it loves what it does
But it's always been inflated by golden bounty within
That strange vessel that is my heart
It takes on so many unknown passengers
Sentiments sink in deep enough to anchor
Some may not understand why it keeps adding more
Making the choice to take on what could be left behind
But my heart is a strange vessel
It only travels where the tide teaches
Only rides where the river runs
Only wanders where the wind wishes
There is no striking this sail
No port alluring enough to put in
Sometimes a buoy, sometimes a beacon
This strange vessel that is my heart

JRE
2011

The main line to this piece was written in 2003, but never became a part of anything substantial. Several years of life experience helped it find a home.

Reflection

I can't decide the look in her eyes
Warm skin waits the eternal moment
A smile slides and I see from the inside
What she knows is left untold

Waiting whispers that keep their secrets well
Intrigue swells into new beginnings
Her laughter lights up the life I lost
Linger my lucky loneliness no longer

Temptation burns underneath a magnetic touch
Fired by the mirrored moments of our lives
To place my whole world in her depths
As she becomes the softest part of me

JRE
2007

I remember that this one came so easily. To me, it's just passion incarnate. It's amazing what can exist between two people. Definitely one of my favourites.

Trust

I'll put my heart down before you
Stab at it
I'll show you that your knife is dull
It matters only in the mind
A matter of the heart
My light is more than your dark

JRE
2004

This was written for someone close to me who didn't consider their friends to be earnest.

Tricky

You have such delicious magic
Enchantment picks me from the audience
The long captivating spell has been cast
Sets swarms in my head, sends swells through my heart
All this from the rabbit under your hat
Your charm has completely overwhelmed
The performance closes with magnificent applause
A volunteer waits outside with a rose and a compliment
But this magic trick is yet to take its proper bow
Swirling colour travels from the darkness
There's a vision of you before me
My words tumble out at your feet
Hope says these words will find you
Prayers tell me what you will say
But your illusion fades into shadow
I'm left alone in the dark
A symphony of crickets
Still waiting

JRE
2011

This was a 2005 piece that I dressed up for the show. Something about the hoped for, but not to be, kind of love. Love can be a tricky fellow.

The Dawn of Dusk

Follow the sweet scent that hints the name
An easy entrance lures you out of the darkness
It's come to grant ambition as well as permission
A silk hand points to purpose and the insight of all
Here is where we find the future

Follow the soft voice that whispers the name
A gentle punishment for the impurity on a clean soul
Convalescence forgets the dirt that did so long reside
A humble modesty flaunts its victory when vanity's conquered
Here is where we forget the past

Follow the sentimental eyes that see the name
Take the offered serenity, but then pass it to another
Sharing evolves into the rapture old pages promised
Love is now an anomaly and is a force upon the wind
Here we ride the wish that propels our present

JRE
2004

Here is a piece about collective possibilities, and people moving toward more prosperous times. It has been slightly reworked from its original form.

Sunrise

She opened her eyes to the sun
Forgot how bright it is. The light in her eyes
Long had it been since megalomania first took her light
Since the dark and the red had taken root
Insidious – the tactic that moved against her soul
And with grip so tight and invited, it advanced toward control

She closed her eyes to the pain
Refused to see it rot. The truth was what she thought
Long had it been since she told them of love
Since she spoke of everlasting and the design of fate
Broken – the worst fear that owned it all
And with an agenda of ignorance, the choice to fall

She blinked her eyes in disbelief
Denial of things lost. Lost within herself
Long had it been since she'd discovered the drain of emptiness
Since loneliness had made a target of her heart
Escape – the only option accepted in this self-inflicted hell
And with intention so defined, 'new' now casts its spell

She opens her eyes to the sun
Realization shines in her eyes. A child of the universe
Long had it been since she knew the light in her heart
Since she'd seen the smiles behind the clouds
Freedom – her chosen chains break in this flight from old
And with the love of fate, she sails and says what needs to be told

JRE
2004

This was written for a friend who had come to a critical juncture in her life. I particularly like how the ending to each second line can be interpreted in different ways.

Stars Crossed

I must have been the one who promised me you
No decent person would make anyone wait this long
I've waited my life's time for someone who understands
And the universe will run out before my sand

I beg gravity to grant its best momentum
My faith is defined by the word 'her'
Anything else leaves me the long lonely fate
And entire empires rise and fall whilst I wait

I wear a disguise over my true eyes
Saving my mated soul for that heavenly promise
I stare out my blue windows watching our time shrink
And absolute galaxies burnout before I blink

I would make every irony for us
It makes the kind of sense that only the stars know
Every beat of my heart is payment for either your truth, or my lie
And a flower's love of the sun is diminished before I

I write this only to make the promise - our promise - real
Shakespeare was never so cruel to his star-crossed lovers
Say our love is only locked away waiting for its surprise
And infinity will finally perish the day she arrives

JRE
2011

Birthed from a 2003 piece, this is about how young love can't get old if it never happens.

Only One Girl

The full moon sky drops a Sicilian thunderbolt
And the possibility rains down from your heavens
Your vision climbs up my eyes and shouts the magic word
Raised stakes and laid hands revealing every ace
Just another drink after the last one and we'll be on our way
Drunk passion drives home with sublime taste already trickling
Find a holy place to park and ravish the chance for something more
Gravity's hard, inebriated grasp trumps a sober man's thoughts
Now my heart only knows what it wants when it's in you

Quick deliverance somehow draws out the flavour scream
We've been dangled over danger and we took the plunge
This midnight lingers long enough to leave a little blood
And consequence shall come for what the full moon saw
A gasoline stain floats on the surface of our love puddle
Solutions put hands in their pockets and whistle away

A diabolical debacle of a dive into our death
My life was swept away in those moments
But this prayer would risk everything I am for you
Some bizarre devotion to putting myself inside the Girl
What we've become is something beyond compulsion
Now fate for us can only be faith for me
After all, there really is only one Girl

JRE
2011

This is an amplification of a 2004 piece. The original was written after a crucial juncture in a rocky "relationship" with a certain someone.

... And My Mind's Made Up

Spilling out like a flood, my expression lacks precision
You are my mind...
I trade my security for suggestion, wash myself in dreams
A lonely heart dictates my direction

Sloppy speech to your ears, explaining my Picasso painted heart
You are my mind...
I fade into my affection, erase my racing pulse
Forceful faith is somehow in command

Slippery with wet words, off target tantrums of truth
You are my mind...
I make memories of your touch, hide myself in hope
Unlock the chains that hold back this beast

JRE
2004

A take on how confessions of love are quite often more convoluted than necessary.

Captured

Time is a red rose petal recovery
Slumber tracks in the snow of life
Tastes of fathomed phantom flavours
And an overwhelming allure of almighty avarice
Witness the done deed of capital crime's chaos
Lambasted little boy brags in a dust covered envelope
Starry grain bolsters a naked lantern over these pages
As chivalry calls for a perpetual wish of melodic march
A slippery string rush of Vivaldi in the spring
Morsels and fragments of some imaginary rainbow
Vanquished by pulsar shards and waves of jellyfish hypnosis
Combinations of sandpiper tracks and soul-mated incantation
Lusty luck lures the nurtured nemesis from this vessel
A sunset smashed in splattering spreads of stained glass
Showered by glowing ember streams of spark dust
Vials of ethereal opiates appear in this utterance
Injecting the hard dose of dream driven divine dive
Swan song that's sprayed on the fields of deliberation
Another shredded jungle of rocks and onyx bits
Yin-yang yawns of ironic ink breed on this paper
Everlasting zero-hour for a voluptuous warranty
Culminations of convalescence and cancelled cancer
The last sight of this world is a marble zenith
And a violet comet of tumultuous verse

JRE
2011

This was spawned from a piece written in 2009. The original seemed so unfinished and beckoned for more. It's become a random collection of imagery and moods from my day to day life, as well as a personal favourite.

Possibly Pathetic

Paint me pretty with a privileged promise
Plucking the past from our powered pride
A perfect panic of this permanent pleasure
It ploughs the pain from new peaceful passions
Then planted pixies in your pampered prison
They've plotted and planned for the prissy prance
Our pleasing, patient, and packaged pestilence
Now purchased by our popular parents so proud
Our once playful purpose pours out pointlessly
As people are plastered by the polished prank
Puddles of our poisoned and pragmatic problems
All the pungent piles of plunder in practice
Poised and pregnant with the pretentious piousness
That pillages the prize from the permissive populace
Now the poor are prodded into positions so pervaded
Their plight will persist until prowess does provide
As the prolific pastures pound with song so percussive
Behold the probable plunge of the potent into purgatory

JRE
2008

This quickly became a tangent that is meant to be somewhat prophetic. (As a person who sometimes spits when he talks, this one can get pretty slippery. 79 P's, that's a 237 in Scrabble.)

Reflex Reflects Choice

Another day begins as another dream ends
Sometimes the hard part is telling the difference between
So many moments to collect all these feelings
Not enough heart to choose the ones worth believing
A strange world it is for you
One that knows and one that shows
But some secret gravity pulls you into the real world
You try to remember what you're looking for
What you find is a place that is safe and warm to stay
So hopeful to learn about true courage
Blindly wishing to learn about divine wisdom
Not the slightest idea of what the journey really is
Dream up delusion and scream confusion before you see
Truth can be found in any insane mind
Careful not to use someone else's measuring stick
Ask yourself the questions, and others if you choose
The answers are all out there waiting
The curiosity, the quest, these are up to you
Pain can be rampant on this trek into the white-light life
Luckily a heart can only be broken if it was all together in the first place

JRE
2003

One of these lines was first written in 1998. In 2003 I put the main piece together. It was originally written with someone else in mind, but after a time I realized it was written for me. This has been reworked again since its initial creation. It's about the desire to come to the end of the hardest journey in life, but how that journey is the one that will never end.

Backstroke

Time drips from its leaky faucet
Just a faint sound splashing in the puddle below
Each drop a bitter reminder, one could drown in this pool
The water's four feet high and rising
It's all too easy to choke on this unnoticed flow
And the chance to act is as delicate as a hanging bubble
Cold water licks your throat as you crane your neck to the ceiling
Alas, too many fleeting moments have flushed these lives away
Time surrounds and sinks any one of us
Time drains anyone who can't swim

JRE
2011

This finished product is an expansion to a 2005 piece. Quite simple, this piece is about how time tends to slip away from us.

Vs.

Life can be so dirty, and the dirt seems to show on you
You've tried so hard to wash it off you've scrubbed to blood and bone
Now dirt goes so very deep, deeper than most know
How far down would you dig to clean up your life's mess?
To sparkle as if brand new, to shine enough to reflect
Underneath is innocence enough for angels to love and keep you
Fear the dirt may dry again, even as you wash in tears?
Plunge into a bath of torturous memories to clean up again
But once your head is soaked, try to see what really lies beneath
This dirt does not belong to you, and dirty have you never been
This mess belongs to someone else and they should keep it
Let them have their stained lives as you see your own clean skin
Flaunt your gorgeous self that comes from both outside and in

JRE
2005

This piece is about the human tendency to carry the sinful deeds of another as our own. It's meant to show that, difficult as it may be, these deeds should be observed, forgiven and laid to rest.

Girl Talk

The sunset sky on my face
In this moment, my passion place
No more night and only this dawn
Laughter's the sound of my favourite song
And although I suspect it is still not time
Her lips and her eyes I wish mingled with mine

JRE
2008

You can't hurry love. No, you just have to wait. Isn't that what Mama said?

Kiss Me Kill Joy

I had a dream
A dream where you came to me
And you touched me
Touched me the way only a woman can
Took me softly
Took me wilfully
But most of all, you took me completely
We went to the place where we always wish
And in that place we had our kiss
Then you put me in a place I'd forgot
And our skin had finally found its peace
Then into you I gave myself
As you accepted with a smile
And so there it was that we forgot our fears
Just for a little while

JRE
2005

This is one of my personal favourites. Based on an actual dream and written within seconds of waking from it. The piece is named for the dream's love interest, one of her many aliases.

In Bloom

The dew glimmers in the fading moonlight
Darkness soaks up the memory and tears
Black so full and bloated it's bursting
Screams from the shrinking shadows
Secrets from behind the silent window
Creeping crimson stretches from the deep
Crooked fingernails scratching the surface
Reaching for what they left behind

Streams of sun from heaven and horizons
Silver light streaks like slivers through the fog
The cloak of night clings to the waking world
Yet ethereal eyes open to penetrate and banish
No more torn curtain hiding things in the night
Magic spells born from old tears and dry blood
The new day starts with a rainbow and a smile
Followed so closely by the truth and its light

JRE
2005

This piece is about the troubling experiences some people go through in life and shows that there's always a chance at a happy ending.

Phantom Love

A stiff and solid situation comes between us
It's made to be this way
Deep down we know it has to be this way
Not so random thoughts stare at the jealous touch
Who's reaching for someone warm in the dark?
Who has the sweetest mistake on their mind?
Decision sinks in a pool of heavy, viscous logic
Buried by the drenching weight of these depths
So much hidden behind a curtain of bright eyes
Almighty appeal drenches a most ravenous idea
The booming voice drawls on so long about guilt
Who knows where the cautions come from?
Who urges the catastrophe of concealment?
This denied love is merely protection
An inflamed scar that shouts the loudest warning
Fear is the poison that makes this ill
Fear is the armour that rusts
Everything we did was all to make him wrong
Our truth suppressed by our ever-to-endure friendship
A lie that only delivers our false fate and a reckoning
Heart-ache scrambles when severance is strapped to a finger
Laid out dreams of a family that feels the fanciest flow
Confessions of the heart cannot overcome that beautiful hair
And that sweet song you sang fades in the chatter
Whose footsteps are headed for the door?
Who's packed and ready for a goodbye?
Tea leaves and tears on the sadness of a spring afternoon
The finale to a truth and dare from another decade
A would-be kiss that only ensures the longest farewell
The thickest cord to be stripped down to the thinnest thread
And as we walk away we leave more than a friendship behind
Our love is a ghost, wandering this world deaf, dumb, and blind
JRE
2011

> A fairly large edit of a 2005 piece, this is written for the unexplored possibility of love between two extremely close friends. The piece evolved over time, with new sentiments being added to the old.

Pinch at Your Peril

I live in an imaginary place
A place where reality is twisted into a dream
My dream
Where illusions are my friends and without them I am bitter
Without them I am alone
This dream keeps and holds me
It medicates my sorry self
As I drift away on my floating fiction I offer no resistance
For here is salvation
Here is my truth
Only here in this dream are you real

JRE
2006

Here I tried to express the sometimes overwhelming desire to exist in the imagination rather than reality. For some people it's easy to make up something more pleasing than the truth.

Opposites React

Laughter loves its birth each day
Sorrow fears when it's gone away
Peace forgives each vindictive heart
War hates when it's torn apart
Harmony accepts the ones who stray
Chaos is angered when it cannot play
Benevolence understands when it doesn't win
Malevolence is confused when it cannot sin

The laughter of love is peace in a forgiving heart
The sorrow of fear is known in war's hateful start
Harmonious understanding is accepting benevolence
Anger is chaos that can be confused with malevolence

JRE
2009

I really like the idea behind this piece. I think it adequately illustrates how negatives depend on negatives, and positives build on positives.

A Party In 1999

The time has come yet again
Get up and get down. Just get it on
Dance into Destiny itself
You can feel the energy grow
Move your body, lose your mind
Feel it in your bones, blood, and soul
Let it take control
The bass will beat you
It beats everyone

Slide and glide in your own stompin' groove
It comes again to set us free
It wants to fall in love
A rush so good can take its toll
Swarming in your head, taking your breath
What goes up must come down
So you gotta show it what you got
Love every beat of it, hear every minute of it
Here we go, nothing can stop it now

Nothing like the Feeling
Party Time – Dance Dance Dance

JRE
1999

This is the oldest piece in the collection, written in November 1999 just hours before attending an all-night rave. Of the hundreds of writings I did in that time of my life, this is the only one coherent enough to print. (At least the only one in my possession.)

A Friend In Me?

There's a stranger wandering through my veins
He's painting the world with some peculiar dream
But everything looks so fake and has no taste
There's a rockstar choking in the background
He's drowning in my ecstasy

There's some stranger running through my head
I don't even know this guy but he says he's my friend
But his face doesn't seem at all familiar
There's a child crying in the corner
His sulking is a funeral

There's this stranger leading me by the hand
He's just so pretty as he flips his candy my way
But his grip is mighty firm for a friend
There's a face in a distant mirror
He's who used to be me

JRE
2011

This was written as a look back on some blurry years in my life.

Pledge

I'm injected with that certain flavour
Pumped full and bloated with the frivolous
Illusions swarm and try to convince me
Please help me chase them away
Flush the folly from my veins and forgive again
I know you do, and I trust you're there

I'm wandering naked in the cold
Amped up with the juicy, runaway train
Dirty hands clutch at my staggering shuffle
Please save me and send them away
Bless my life with the thickest gravy
You're always listening, you're always around

I'm in the dark chopping through the woods
Strung up on notches higher than heaven
Sinister fellows are telling me those nasty stories again
Please don't let me forget you now
Project on me a whole rainbow of lights
You always said you loved me, you promised

JRE
2008

This was written in 2008 but is thinking on a time in my life several years earlier. It's about the appeals and prayers a person can make for redemption but how, most times, a person ignores the help they receive and cause their own relapse.

The Worn Tracks of Yesterday

Oh lost song of the night
Oh beautiful stars that shine
Your memory taunts my time
And I feel your tingle, twinkle touch
I miss you so much

Oh sweet song of the night
Oh wishing stars that wink
Your rainbow ride will only sink
And I dance on your pill granted rush
I fear morning's hush

Oh precious song of the night
Oh reigning stars that con
Your spell's drip holds off the dawn
And I suck your moon's forever kiss
I buy death with bliss

Oh glorious song of the night
Oh triumphant stars that sing
Your high has bitter ending
And I cringe at your sour, sickly skin
I see now your sin

JRE
2008

Another piece written in 2008 that thinks back on earlier years, 1999 - 2002, when raves were all the rage (at least for me).

Emancipation Determination

Black and hard with gray
Cracked crust, dusty skin
You shudder as your mask breaks
And you give up your secret

Light in the shadow, day over night
You cannot deny the sacred flight
The erupting dry and dirty face
No longer do prisoners reside in this place
Focus flickers in once warm core
Frozen cold ash is dead no more

Shatter the suffering
It's been far too long
You surrender the time you took
And you free the captive you held

Splendid time of sweet rebirth
Rise up now casting off the curse
Damaged dreams no longer slumber
Returning home to the sacred mother
Fire flashes where once was death
Life is alive and again has breath

JRE
2008

This piece comes from the beginning of a transitional phase in my life. It expresses the desire to climb out of a rut and leave old troubles behind.

After the War

I see with no sins for I am blinded by lies
But the dishonesty I thought yours is plainly mine
Written off to the carnage of chemical assaults
Infected infant choices throttle my heart
The future is immersed in this fallout
And I wonder what now defines me
Poison still runs thick in my veins
Medicated memories touch me from the distance
Mournful screams echo in the darkness all around
It's a mad scramble to ascend from this travesty
Running from what was once seen as the saviour
A life has been devastated by a sedated command
Silence has so much work to do
Silence will hurt no more

JRE
2011

The first line of this piece was written 1998 and, to my recall, is the first thing I ever wrote. (At least the first of any real substance.) The rest of this didn't come until much later. The finished result is a reflection on the aftermath of the decisions made in my youth.

Remedy

With every breath I am taking my thoughts drift back to you
With each beat my heart is making I learn things I never knew
You've taught how the light inside is easily hidden or dimmed
But no one can extinguish that light for it's something we hold within
You've shown me a world of wonders and given me a taste
A sample of what life can be for those who don't spill or waste
For every dream I've forgotten you've given me ten more to know
For every hope I've abandoned you've planted a seed to grow
I never knew what I was missing until you came with your touch
How could I ever have questioned a life that offers so much?

JRE
2002

One of my earliest pieces, this came together when I found a friend in someone I'd avoided for years. This piece was written in a time of intense convalescence. Sometimes I think it's a little too "Hallmark". However, it means too much to me to change and risk its original meaning.

Next of Kin

Time is come and time is gone
I laugh as the sand falls through my fingers
Not a laugh of joy, but a laugh of ridicule
Sneering in the face of what I thought I was
It's fitting now, quite fitting
It's proper to laugh at a joke
So much has faded yet still residual
Left behind and hiding

Remnants of an old shield
Broken pieces with jagged, icy edges
Cutting their way through my life
Through all my time
My lacerations leaking
Spoils and stains on new designs
Scars are the bitter reminder
My own personal stigmata

From a puddle of deepest red on a far away hill
I drag myself through the dust and dirt
And lo, here is where forgiveness finds me
Light dangles its glorious self over my corpse
Someone steps out from inside me to identify
Bright eyes look me over with a frozen face
He doesn't betray remorse with even the slightest flinch
Funny, I thought I was the one who got away

JRE
2011

This piece is an extension to another originally written in 2005. It revolves around an alias I had for several years in my life. It's written at the point where the true self becomes aware of the alter-ego and acts, but is intentionally vague as to whose perspective we're reading.

Freehand

This pen, once dropped, never writes again, these words never writ before
When a silent hush holds the world, the pen can rule once more
And how these words find their place still amazes me
And yet these words form writings, and what they write sets me free

JRE
2003

This tries to express a feeling that my poetry is an essential outlet for me, and that sometimes I don't even know how I write it, or where it comes from.

Star of Wonder

Found within a dream I had a meaning oh so clear
Whispers of a shining star that tells us all our fears
It speaks in twisted riddles and tells us what's undone
It beckons us to follow as it guides us to the sun
A star that shines so bright, that's always been left alone
It's waiting for us to swallow so the true light can be shown
And in the dream you should've seen the light that shone in my eyes
Of things unseen and not believed, I saw through every lie
So the star told me what could come to be if we could all stop fearing truth
But it also said something so sad, that as humans we always need proof

JRE
2002

Another early piece, I remember writing this and feeling a great sense of fulfillment for how easy and unforced it emerged.

Hear Here

Grazing in a daze for days in this maze
Just stumbling as the crumbling is all so troubling
Trying, not crying, but still my time's flying
Where my worn wear is worn and torn
They trick me quickly and prick me but don't flick me
Draw a dripping drop of slipping red blood shot
They see the stranger in the manger as danger
And run stunned and arm their denial guns
Praying to keep their creeps and reap what you sleep
Protect the captured rapture that's manufactured with fracture
It's the muzzled puzzle that they'll gluttonously guzzle
Hear here, pass the past and last passed the mass
Surpassing lies and alibis are the eyes that rise
Only they who drink the river shall link before the brink
Soon the cooing dove soars high above wooing our love
Her sounding song is such a touch of so much, too much
Singing of living and giving and that no giving is no living

JRE
2008

A look at the way things are all around me, and a voice inside reassuring me about the world's constant changes.

New Life Now

Awake the child within
Become the infant I've always been
Curiosity is my cure
Innocent wonder makes me sure
Embrace the first time I ever taste
Love without a double-thought trace
Pristine skin, soft smooth chin
Everything around me brand new begins
The immortal puzzle that is my mind
Everyday dawns a puzzle piece find
Eternal lessons without preconception
Unrestricted perfection in beautiful perception
Every choice that's yet to become
Every outcome that's so far from done
So many questions with infinite time
All the answers with no need to be mine
Travel to wisdom with pure heart so full
Not one moment waiting, doleful or null
Swell up old child and make yourself new
A just out of heaven perspective is you

JRE
2008

This is about freeing the child within, the simple innocence that somehow gets locked away inside as life goes on. Adults tend to forget how pure life can be because they've been doing it for so long. It takes a special mind to remember what it's like to do things and see things for the first time.

Somatose

I am reborn in a dangerous room
It tempts the travesty in me
These aged reasons are wrapped and tangled
And they dangle on a bloated vine of desire
Stretch the mirror until it shows me your deepest reflection
The immaculate picture taken in the night of day
Criminal culminations find fruit enough to suckle
But we linger on in your forbidden realm
In the negated space of thoughtless forevers
Death is too expensive, so you slip it in your pocket
Sneak your demise under the scrupulous eyes of the blind
But it's a burden that you've stitched into your crime
Extinguish the glowing embers of a sacred bonding
You've stifled the pale hope of infants yet to come
And banished them with the sentences you toss like candy
Who's burnt the bridge from the wrong side?
But I'm the sulking mourner of these charred ashes
My tattooed time is wounded by the knife you flail
And the shadow class has me in their clutches
Someone tell me if we have anything that lasts
What the man on the prison says is fake and putrid
It seeps into my soul and drills for more permission
The distribution of the only real disease
Contaminated delivery direct to our doors
Free infections for the faithful listeners
Our favourite smiles pat our empty heads
And we crawl on down the hall
Seek redemption in that old dangerous room
Only to dry up like a desert
But come give us a better ending
Grant the last wish of these happy people
Tell them there is a word that will save them

JRE
2008

The gist of this is the perversion of what was once sacred, and how very few of us notice or care.

Salvation

As the rapture comes with its cost, I'm shown the life to be
And if the world's shown me what we've never seen, it means I've never been lost

JRE
2007

I've often thought about adding to this but I always end up feeling like it would mute the point. In my view, this speaks the truth I felt in one of life's special moments and, like all real truth, it shouldn't have anything else attached to it.

Lovely

I travel to and through the truth
Only to find that I have always been
I seek to save and sanctify my soul
Only to see that it has always been
I search for love in places I've never seen
Only to remember that love has always been
My sweet recall of precious memory
Every joy that sets the world free
The future's now and it lights the way
I see that I am the emerging truth
I remember that I am your body
I believe in the greater human heart
I stand as one with the forgotten son
I love us all as we all once did
Our life becomes the heavenly horizon
We all knew this to be true
I am love, you are love
And I love you, Love, too

JRE
2008

Expressed here is my personal belief that life is more of a remembering process than a learning process. When I feel these memories inside it always makes me feel so connected.

Everessence

Sopping puddles leak from pine tree gullies of green shade
Beacons of white birch blow in hope-winds on a hillside
A tall glass of immaculate sun pours through a veiled sky
Bluest purple clouds gather the purity as it gushes from heaven
The frost-silver forest falls into the memory of our spinning orb
Its thirst quenched and satisfied by the melting snow drops
Dew drenched in a baptismal of celestial overcast
Earth motions melded into solid purpose for the equinox sun
The strings of electric webs against gray-blue curtains
A melange of melancholy chords and heart strings
Vibration stirs this cauldron of molten dreams
Chrysalis of slumbering soul pregnant and poised
The red grass moon beseeches the stars for a swift twirl
A new earth made of blossoms and butterflies in honeybee fields

JRE
2011

This piece is based on impressions instilled in me by a glorious morning of early spring.

Elephant Shoe

The tapestry of my life, it unravels to reveal
The secrets of forgotten times, and memories that once were real
My hungry heart consumes me, swallows my reason whole
Here I'll chew myself tonight, and let heart now eat my soul
I capture time with my eyes, I say I can't let go
And as time slips by, I wait and cry
For the words I am never told

JRE
2007

Loneliness can be its own worst enemy... or in this case, a muse.

Absence

My lonely eyes see only shadows
Light won't reach this wretched place
Where strange thoughts become stranger words
The mornings of memory are for me tomorrow
And I do this all on purpose

Almighty illusion caresses my anxious time
To void the fear of what this can only be
Locked and latched like the life I choose
And I do this just to write these words

Clockwork clicks
Alarm bells ring
But this slumber just goes on
Absence is mother to these words
Absence is a sparkling invitation

JRE
2007

Here my poetry is blamed for a bad mood. I try to express how we often suffer needlessly, and by our own hand.

Barking

Malevolence mangled on a morning of mucky moon
Survivors surrender at the sight of those sneaky snails
Flailing faiths fall to the fake pharmacy fates
Tummies tucked triple in the terrible torrents of truth
Quick while the quacks are quietly quoting coughs
The losers lick up the lies from the large lazy lake
A pissed-off prattle of puffy, pregnant pawns
Never known nothings with their no-no nukes

JRE
2008

I read this and think I'm either barking mad or just barking like a dog. Or perhaps I should just redouble my efforts to avoid the TV news.

Daily Dose

The star in the night yields to the morning sun
Just a brief moment of ignorant bliss before reality turns on
Her life hits her, and she scrambles for the fix
She guzzles down the fiction that keeps her safe
Swallows her entire fairy tale whole
But she'll reach for another dose to be sure
We can't have the truth around here

The sun and the horizon say their farewells
For just a moment the pain seeps through the cracks in her courage
Catastrophe enters the room with a bold shove
The bastard with such a loud, obnoxious voice
Teeth grit and neck twinge as she clutches madly for the bottle
Drink it down to spare the truth an embarrassment
We wouldn't want to see something so ugly

The sun embraces the coming twilight and soon the moon
One quick moment of peace as the daylight dims
Ruined with the realization that tomorrow will do it again
Then it's out for the night to seek fuel for the myth
Hold still dear fellow and choke on this kiss
She'll soon be off to bed with her liquid lies
We won't be seeing anything tonight

The lonely star reigns over the black
One long moment that holds sway over all others
Deliverance is granted with a sweet dream slumber
She finds herself in a sedated daze of gooey truth
Redemption speaks, but only to her unconscious self
And a star tells her it's time to come home
We shan't be seeing her anymore

JRE
2011

This was carved out of a 2007 piece. Essentially it's about how some people live a lie and become so addicted to their lie they live by nothing else.

The Cracked Cocoon

The many tired times that pick away at our life
Silent nights haunted by the harsh words under the sheets
Slumber that is not to be, for the jaded opinion sleeps here
Cunning art of tip-toe treatment to save just one moment
What talent in a dried up poet and a forgotten artist
Frustration comes from the dark side of our beautiful sunset
A festered ferment of the thickest discontent boils and stews
Forbidden, silent secrets creep out of a weak, clumsy heart
Forgotten, stale words can still sting like a slithering sliver
A painfully empty shell that was once home to so much more

JRE
2011

This finished product emerged from a 2008 piece. A break-up inspired the original. I'd like to mention that this piece once had a happy ending. That ending was removed merely for dramatic effect, not over hard feelings... of which there are none.

Murdered Muse

Crab apples grow on the hope tree
The dawn cannot find this place
There is no sun to share
She trickles down into the drain of memory
And all the flooding words are dammed by our death
I run from her corpse clinging to the remnants
Keeping only the best parts
But the shadow of my steps follows me down
It demands those magnificent words
It's punished with a scowl as I oblige
But the figure fades without reply
And now there is no more
The long silk hair that my fingers possessed
Run it like a river through my desperate recall
Pull the picture from yesterday's gallery
Just a shimmering trace of that sleek summer song
My words are broken without that shine
My broken words have never been so sublime

JRE
2008

This piece is about how certain people tend to inspire more than others and how it might be unwise to depend on such inspiration. This has become a personal favourite.

Necrosis

A dose of triumphant mourning
Carried off to the lonely chamber
Plunge into warm, wet sweetness
A vital recital of passionate skin
Wrapped in a sweaty blanket of denial
A ghost creeps into the love thicket
Hungry evil is under these sheets
Determined desire fulfills its will
A veil of black shrouds this nest
Drained of the nectar of new life
Sacrificed on the altar of night
Awake without a reason to stay
Leave behind what could never be

JRE
2008

This is a piece about what happens when a break up is dragged out passed that certain crucial point.

Not Away Saga

I know this place so well
It feels like before I forgot
Returns to me without effort
Waters of my youth refresh
Waves wash away the recent
I am bathed in precious time
Memory is a pink stormy sunset
Midnight dips itself in cold waters
Rushing rain rises out of soft sand
Castles of mud ruled by my hand
Family was carved in these stones
I was raised on this white shore
Baptized by these sacred, serene waters

JRE
2008

This is about returning to the memories of childhood, in both body and mind. The title is wordplay for the place that inspired me.

Permission Radio

My selected radio fills my head as it fills my day
Buzzing through my ears are the tunes I choose
I built this station before I knew what music was
Tuned my dial to what was all around me
And I turned purposefully away from the popular

My selected radio fills my mind as it fills my dreams
Rampaging through my family are the tunes I choose
I built my life on what this music proclaims
Deaf to any dial that was different
And I walked away from the suggestions and invites

My selected radio fills my hands as it fills my time
Pounding through my body are the tunes I choose
I built an altar and worshipped this music
All those dials were tuned to me
And I danced until I was lost in dark oblivion

My selected radio fills my eyes as it fills my screen
Skimming through my mind are the tunes I choose
I built a library of the undiscovered music
So many dials to tune to all at once
And I listened to everything that I'd never heard before

My selected radio fills my heart as it fills my life
Echoing through my soul are the tunes I choose
I built this freedom because music has no limits
Let the dial go to tune itself
And I follow my trail in life to the music that makes me feel
JRE
2011

> This piece is about my ever-changing taste in music, and how important it is to remain open to all types of music. When I was young I took such a set against certain kinds of music, wasting years denying genres only to finally relent. Now some of my favourite music is the kind my teenage self would spend a lifetime ignoring.

It's Genetic

As our opened eyes come to an end, that's when he rubs you in
Instantly on the loose, you track with perfection
You're no more than a precise clap and soft punches at first
It's when you're at your best. Open our eyes and you agree so well
I feel you start to take over as you box in your beat
Suddenly his fingers give a slick flick and there's a kick
Though it's not the kick that brings you to life, but a sneaky trickle
Well just strut right in and make yourself at home
It's a diabolical dilemma of four count delight
A blatant and dynamic dance of disruption that's got it all in the background
You pile on each new gear and give us high-ended satisfaction
In between the fingered notes and the highs and lows, a long coil rises
That kinked groove climbs out of the midrange
Twisted and tangled in its captivating delivery
And you climb higher and higher until you're too much
Soon it's all we can take, and you dive
The easy brakes that give way, and a cymbal sizzles into thunder
You leave us with the soft touch, that gentle sin with the electric tease
And the long string starts to pull, tighter and tighter bringing you all together
Cast the long spell – Give us thunder as the midrange rains
Still rising, laying it on thick – Still rising, glazing double quick
Fit in some quick claps – You deserve the applause as thunder and midrange reigns
Gallop up the slope and give into the winding whirlwind
A perfect pleasure of divine sin delivers one more thunder roll
It gets so easy that all could fade away – But no, you whine and curl into that fetal ball
Instead you send a high pitched siren and present a sneaky crescendo
It all comes back to us now, the fine grind – Your energy is a raw, unchallenged storm
That distinct drive that dazzles my destiny with a force indescribable
And as you charge on, your mighty coil rides the air
But even you are too good to last forever, and you begin to give way
It's the final chance at your diabolical plot, but you keep your promise
As you drop into that final break he releases the next beast and it's already on the hunt
And when you explode out of your silence, heaven's scent is on the air
JRE
2011

A play by play overview of "Genetic" by Activa, as it appears on Eddie Halliwell's Cream Ibiza Mix '07.

My Spacey Place

This night passes with runny-make-up tears
The stains on once white tissue seem to mingle with the moment
Truth is defined with a whisper as love escapes out the cold and broken window
Scattered, shattered shadows break the light and show the insipid color
"Time has found us, time has found us". The mantra in my mind
Here I sleep with the delusion dreams that will soon own my morning
There is crimson in my eyes, there is crimson in my veins
Medicate this vessel and let me see with real eyes
Are you waiting for me? Are you looking for me?

JRE
2006

This spilled out onto my old My Space page one day. I started typing and this is what the words said when I was done.

Cradle My Child

It seems so much of my life has been lost to time
Time that takes every attempt of my goodness and keeps it from me
Keeps me away from the destiny I strive for everyday
And everyday becomes my same miserable excuse of nothingness
Now I ask myself for permission. Grant me take it back
Give up all those old faded moments. Give myself back to me

It's alright now, sweet child. No need to hide in the dark
Come out to play. See the world and love the day
The life you thought lost was shattered not. Never broken
Each step and each stage, everything was all for a better phase
Now then, soft child, take this hand and come into the sun
Greet your love and honour the Goddess in all her splendour
The wind, the rain, the earth and fire; hold them in your heart
These are the gifts that show you life and fuel your journey
My pattern and path are yours, my child. Walk with me now
Do not be afraid and do not run away. This time is ours everyday
Today's dreams hang on a rope called tomorrow, so not a moment to lose
My darling child, only you can choose to ignite this forgotten life
Make the promise to yourself and feel my arms cradle you
My strength pounds on the door to your heart
Sweet child, you need but only answer

JRE
2008

This piece is about the need to forgive oneself, and putting your faith in the right place.

The Modern Age

Maximized miracles on the Who's God channel
Special little sins for children in flannels
Plastic puppet talent on bazillions of stations
Don't pick that jerk as the leader of our nation
Thumbed up movies about Jews being gassed
Bleeped out faggots from thirty years passed
Spoon fed margarine from the human trough
I hate this show, someone please turn it off
Supersized chemistry for meals and snacks
False flag televised terrorist attacks
Mother Nature sporting a 'For Sale' sign
Holy Father Time gives his Rolex a wind
Gospel-stock's up while the Gospel's stock's down
Pave the planet to bypass this town
Warm global concern gets the cold shoulder
Tweet to the world: the apocalypse is over
Simon Science says God isn't the case
Sir Reverend Doctor preaches the pharmacy faith
Cell phone apps that predict epic fails
Huge penis pills put your pelvis on rails
Educated robots recite the long line
Tube tested babies claim eugenics is fine
Family dinner chokes on celebrity juice
Brand name kids are out on the loose
Max the card toward the debt we bought
Doublethink decisions Big Brother taught
Messiah TV broadcasts the brink
Kick back, relax, have a big drink

JRE
2011

This is a large rework of a piece done in 2008. It's meant to be provocative rather than negative.
Personally, I think it's hilarious.

Sunny Tomorrow, With a Chance of Death

Even after all our deeds the sun still finds the earth
Such amazing persistence, and we can only marvel at the feat
Time and time again we dig in our heels, hold our ground, and push
But try as we do to the contrary, the earth will be the one to defeat us
Truly it seems as though the earth has proven to be far too clever for us all
It was nothing but a dirty trick to stash away all this shiny stuff to distract us
Albeit a brilliant, cunning perpetration, but it's just downright unfair of the earth
And while we've been treasuring our made up world, the winds have been whispering

Earth's almighty patience outweighs all the gold we value
Such a dazzling demonstration of where the real wealth is found
Year after year we deal with this day's problems as if plucking leaves on a tree
But we do not listen as the earth asks us to look deeper and examine what lies beneath
As we drown in an ocean of dead leaves, it's the earth that points out the rotting roots to our tree
Surrendering a battle to an enemy is hard enough without the consideration that we are our own enemy
We think we know so much, but the need for perpetual infancy isn't outlined too well in our gospel textbooks
And while we've been writing our own story, the sand of time has been running through our mother's ancient fingers

Our choices are a price tag which the earth will not abide
Such a blatant turning away from the essential source of our lives
Century by century we erode the heavenly body that so graciously lets us reside
But there's no end in sight to our blind march and its home-delivered, super-sized devastation
Ignorance has gleefully invented lifeless things that have more value than the elements required to live
Charging on with belligerent smiles smeared across our well fed faces, throwing angered eyes at the reminders
Our efforts are still set to erasing the few remaining vestiges that connect us to our mother and her bountiful glory
And while we've been playing with fire, the earth's waters have risen, and soon our mother's hand shall wash us clean

JRE
2011

A major edit of a previous piece, this is about western culture's unhindered affront to nature and its ignorance to how a civilization that requires the earth to exist exploits the very thing that grants its existence. The piece suggests that these choices should be stopped and that, one way or another, it will have to end.

The Eagle

He's born by the protection of angels
Walks with God in his pocket
Tells you it is so and shall always be
Teaches anyone with the easy touch
He flies high above the billowing smoke
Honours a child who must carry a hard life
Gives away all that he is to any other
He promises only what can be kept
Believes without any need for proof
Knows the memories that will be the future
He hears and recites the master's voice
Speaks in tongue that few remember
Sees through the eyes of his siblings
He stands beside anyone who would stand up
Comforts the ones who cry in the corners
Rises up to seek out the sore ones
He carries the burdens that belong to us all
Reaches forward with hands of whitest light
Resurrects truth from a long-preached lie
He plants seeds in each and every garden
Rides the bareback of the white horse
Embraces the children we all once were
He holds the hope of the humbled masses
Forgives every trespass against heaven
Redeems the proudest parts of our lives
He trusts us to choose this for ourselves
Invites everyone to feel what is there to feel
And loves with the heart that we all share

JRE

2011

This is based on an actual person I've been fortunate enough to have in my life, a privilege that is honouring and humbling. Perhaps this also touches on what I wish to find within myself, or maybe it even represents the potential in each of us.

Fable

A silk hand dips its fingers in the molten gold of memory
The shiny pool sees the rippling rings sent to horizon tides
Every swell on the shimmering sea started as a hoop with nothing but hope
And it is this wave that washes our most silent history onto the awaiting shore
Just think on the possibilities of all this patience...
Towering echoes of Archangel footsteps shake the vast hallways of heaven
A summons that parts the black curtain-clouds to present a fluorescent firmament
This dawn is God's masterpiece rising from traces and strings of smoke
And our story collides with fate under the watchful glare of the chameleon sun
A dead scarecrow tree caresses these holy ribbons of pink-lit horizon
That wooden spire exposes the forbidden memory we locked in a dark, marble chamber
And we retaliate with an uprising of flashy red skies and remnants of a lightning war
But an anointed phoenix bursts through the colossal oak doors of the ancient library
And by the easy grace of the Lord, the walls of historical deceit are splintered
Dry pages are torn from their sticky sins and flames lick out the deepest crevices
The fallen seethe in the canyon of morals-in-mayhem, and they reach frantically for the light
Desperate times call for despicable men, and they come with their gilded promises
A shiny smile of fake salvation offered up by the red eyes of a metallic messiah
His leaky spillage only quotes the greasy oil of a long broken machine
But his goo seeps its slime into any unarmed heart
Be warned, that story is only the copulation of satin and sin
Hear the truth in this surge of cunning verse as it twists the tale into taste
These words were born in a place where fog is thick
But believe they travel from the halls where orchestral angels abide
From black cherry moons and through the garden of golden autumn
Definitions of divine destiny in the star-strewn abyss
I wrote all this before I came here
By this hand revelations were penned and promised
A saga of sacred chalice pours out a long thread of secrets
Stitched in soul by the lightest touch of exalted eloquence
And now you decide which face will be your General
For in this war, one's faith will be the only armour
But take these words as thy ultimate weapon
As these words have been touched by the hand
JRE
2011

Mastercraft

The kingdom I crave is beyond your thoughts
A dive into the dreamy dominion beyond touch
Basking in an abstract illumination of cherub chorus
A life is a miracle of the moon-drop mind
Designs that mimic angel wings
Mark each soul with your favourite star
Wish on that childhood song
Just one lamb astray from the flock
A candle that burns alone in the dark
All in this together

JRE
2011

This piece was born from another written in 2008. It's about faith and the place I believe we all come from, and return to.

Ego On Auto

Moment by moment is flashes of clear
One now is focused, the next obscure
It's all there inside me, awaking, surging
So much alive, all contained within
Bursting with the truth that is not expressed
Moment by moment I fail my own test

The mask I made, the mask I chose
The face I show off to our world
It speaks first and it speaks last
A force so quick and dominant
I see how it began, witness to old construction
I now seek to undo what so many moments have funded

My choice to make it, my choice to break it
My mask is caught in the light
I can see it, so now I can shed it
Thanks for showing me the way

JRE
2010

This touches on my belief that inside each person are two identities; the ego and the true self. I feel that the ego attempts to control your life but, try as it might, it can never truly be in charge, as the true self uses the ego as an unbeknownst puppet. The second line's usage of the word 'now' refers to "the now", as in the only moment that truly exists. The last line represents the gratitude of the true self towards the ego for its demonstration of what not to be.

Sun Kissed

Leave me in the summer sun
Let cloudy looms spin golden billows
Then show me shine in blue so bright
Where day yields only to the permissive moon
And throw me out into the endless waves
Where a flume flows through mystic fates
Grind me into sandy shores of diamond sand
Spread me out until I am the horizons of green
Then feed me with thunder's tears
And again
Fill me up with that summer sun
The lovely light that ignites my soul
Stretch this body to the soaring mountains
And let my fingers scrape the tallest sky
Evaporate my senses and put me in the wind
Send me from exalted heights to frozen icy lows
Bury me in the caverns where deepest dark resides
But make a promise that the sun will find me there
So I can love and live like this forevermore

JRE
2010

I was trying to show how the great outdoors takes away all other concerns and makes me feel like I have all I need.

Severance

There are so many reasons and I know them all
The endless preponderant burden and buried treasure
Swarm up to my throat and kill or let speak
My dammed heart is ready to flow like a waterfall
White waves ride high in the tide and swallow
The deep plunge that is my rebirth
The capital curse that is my life's work
I am alone as I make myself in my soliloquy mind
Life for me is the distance I keep from the rest
How I need to triumph today for another way
Pass all this by and look to the sky for the other time
I can see our children in the new, green grass
Watch them as they spin and sing and let themselves show
Fragrant flowers in their hair and born of sunlight strands
What masterpiece of man can compare with God's dream?
What human goal or desire can compete with the almighty destiny?
I sail down the river of your incessant torment
Navigate the stars and listen to the wind
Beyond choice and decision is the realm of fate
Where intention and determination meet and find love
Fascinated fancy with the coalescence and togetherness
Is it a dream? Is it a myth? Is it the medication?
Shock me chakra with shimmering shine
Fill me then spill me over all your blind lives
Dip me dancing in water that is wine
Fulfill me completely then dissolve me in time
Are the riddles of life the real life? Ask our angel hearts
Wake from the dream to witness the nightmare
Denial swallows the bitter pill
Truth is the only course to rebirth
Cut the cord
JRE
2008

Written at the peak of a transitional phase in my life, this piece comes from a feeling of new beginning. For me, it's about letting go of things past and finding the courage to take the hard steps. Another personal favourite.

In Perfect Focus

Tricky trouble taxes our time
Sticky cash hand, stabbing needle spine
Coma case of the terminal type
Tube fed fruit that once was ripe
They fade me, flick me – turn me off
Love me, lick me – tell me turn head cough
Diagnose the dangerous with devil driven thoughts
Medicated maintenance for the halves and the knots
Complex promised clarity from silver tongue spew
Come bless my blood as it's bled out for you

JRE
2008

Sometimes you just see things so clearly. Ya know what I mean?

The Sweetness

This absence of touch crawls through the driest desert
How anxious can an animal be to feel the end of a drought?
Beastly instinct collects the scent from every wind
Phantom pheromones declare the obvious almighty
Passion pours from these pores planting the subliminal kiss
And lo, her skin's heard the heavy heat of the night
My long moon howl follows her down to the velvet glade
The crimson river runs as a vampire embrace seizes her succulence
It's not long before pink purity beckons for its true love
The long awaited, eternally insatiable invitation of Her Holiness
Two mortal angels plunge into the artwork of the ancients
Inside the warm, wet cathedral of carnal coalescence
These halls are smeared with the sweetest honey
These walls are soaked with the most saccharine syrup
Love's locked away in a calm castle of holy secrets
Reach beyond the deep blue curtain and find what's inside
Pluck a seed from that sacred granary and plant it in her soil
A sensual slip passed her veil to draw out the slick cider
And one animal angel is drained into another
We curl up in a thick blanket of epic fondness
The temptress has been slaked by moonlit skin
This sweat is a tattoo of triumph over the tantalized
This night is sealed in Mona Lisa smiles

JRE
2011

Spawned from a piece originally done in 2003, I think we all know what this is about. This piece is definitely a personal favourite.

Ray of Sunshine

Sadness is this pen in my hand
When it scribbles these words
These sloppy words that try to flow
Offering what one person can feel
Flicker flame in my mind
Tell the tale of a misplaced life
The sudden shudder and forgotten flutter
My white silk dream is only a shattered mirror
Fantasy flaunts its faded blue collar
Karma is paid by my bleeding heart
Filmy vision shifts to the pointy fingers
So many smiles drown in the sea of tears
Dripping daisy ink has stained these faces
Loneliness is such a blatant tattoo
Haunted stars hear endless insipid prayers
Cuddly chaos suckles at a generous bosom
A suffocation of lies swarm up to swallow
Almighty denial has cast the silent vote
Time is on trial and tried this night
Judgment hides in the dark, unseen corner
And sadness is all this blood on my hands

JRE
2008

Sometimes, when you change your life and move forward passed troubled times, a deep release is required. For me, hardships and harsh feelings all too often get dumped onto paper. On a side-note, I've always thought that a group of lies should be called a "suffocation".

Sick Ink

My inky pollution comes to life
So quick, and at this age it feels anger first
It wants to blather on about insults and slaves
My ink won't kneel down and will not surrender
This pen is a drill, and if given freedom it will act
It's in control when it's out of control
Careful to keep the colour inside the lines
My sick head is spilled onto paper
Swirls and stains of another teenage prisoner

My inky disease returns from the dead
A plague on the tattered pages of my life
Drawling on about excuses and arsenals
My ink would be a plague on all your houses
This pen does only what it's been designed to do
It's in my hand and on the loose
Coaxing the herd from the poisoned waters
My sick head is screaming out at subscriptions
Stars and symbols of another holy advertisement

My inky destiny decides to awake from within
Salvation finds its way into art and expression
It wants to rejoice about escapes and exoduses
My ink shall be an almighty invitation
This pen a key to so many locks and chains
It's in heat and hot to the touch
Climbing the divine ladder of truth
My sick head is sleeping inside these words
Secrets and sacraments of another crazy kid

JRE
2011

Initially I thought to include a piece I'd written in 2000 but, after reviewing the piece and seeing how overly negative it was, I decided not to include it. Instead I wrote a new piece using imagery from the old and crafted a sort of commentary on the older piece. The original, "Sickness of the Head", was written in Mr. Martino's high-school law class.

Expulsion

Tuck loneliness into these tears to purge that bitter gush
Thick streams of muffled screams attached to everlasting tangents
Words wrought with the wretched and gnarled parts of shadows
Syllables drip with the poison that's fermented in a cavernous core
Put pain in a mirror and stare evermore at the me-roar me-roar on the wall
Peeled puppet skin folded gently into origami amusements
Hollowed whole to bolster a stagnant storm of scorching soliloquies
This feral full moon collects its tantrum of fierce, primeval assault
Sour enchantments summon scab dragons from damp, forgotten caves
The ravages leave only the ragged strings of a lowly, tattered heart
A potent prayer comes to say that sunlight shall no longer abide
Crimp the jaded edges of this broken statue with the strongest iron
Cinders and snivels of a vivid demise issued by sinister suggestion
Bled out love on this morning of soggy spring and stained forever
Through the sickest swamp this soul has swum its tedious stroke
And now it scratches itself across the jagged sand of tomorrow
The discarded shell of crabby memory and scum rotted filth
Finally free when there's nothing left for red eyes to swallow

JRE
2011

> I think of this as a cleansing, as if all the darkest parts are poured out in a culmination of brutal negativity. The idea is that after this release only the best bits will remain.

The Coronation of Reflection and Light

I wear my ego like a crown
Treasuring my sight as the heaviest jewel
Raising myself up to the highest seat
To sit upon the thorny throne of judgement
Strapped to this fate with the strongest cords
Relentless, never relinquishing what I've purchased
Wrapping my fingers around this golden prize
Clutching the only thing that makes me more
This lets me carry the weight of the world

I edge into the mirror's range, and gawk
Stunned by the sudden sight of my jealous reflection
I force my eyes open to take in this treason
The man I see seeks what should never be sought
Reach through that thick shell and grab the stickiest weed
Ripping the pollution and machine from my self's center
So now I sift my life through the finest wires
Face the frightening truth that I've carried for so long
A sense and a search for the person who I really am

I hold up a torch against the fear in my shadow
Collect the courage to see what makes the crown cringe
To rise up and challenge the me that I'd want to be
To kneel before the gift of light that's returned
This highlights the areas of the deepest concern
A new sight that sees how to purge what was never real
My facade came to teach me about the last time
Now it's wise drums in a circle of thirteen
And the honour of standing beside the one

JRE
2011

This piece is about how my ego has always tried to control my actions, and how, through a slow and patient process, I seek to shed it and come to realize my true self.

Unicorn

Magic eyes to see this magic world
Sight enchanted by the sight I see
Sail my life from here to that far shore
Sink my feet into the soft sand of forever
I wake up from my dream to remember the myth
The fable of my faith, the blood in my veins
Red river of fate pumps and pounds in my heart
Then destiny's dawn delivers the sweet light in our eyes
Every dream alive in a life that's still waking
Tell me the tale of when we were born
When the golden staircase was in use
Remind me of the hunt and the hunted
Remember all the infinite moments apart
But when the story is dark clouds and accepted loneliness, stop
Just words of what came next could never be enough
I know the next by the beating of my heart
Your starburst eyes have me now. The spell…
And the charm I welcome, for it is my happiest day
The sun's above and the earth still below
Spin after spin, rise to set, set to rise
It's all with you now. The real life
Hold my hand and take my breath.
They've been yours all along
Live what's true, what we always knew
Light up the love that we've found

JRE
2010

This piece was written during that initial phase of a relationship where the connection is like a sizzling rush. The title suggests that this experience can be somewhat mythical and magical.

Fire Within

Another angel asks of me
"Where is your fire, where is your passion?"
It is seen as unseen, a sight unsighted
Proclaimed invisible or nonexistent
An illusion, an apparition
A figment of some other imagination
Sleepless nights, cluttered mind
Wake up to that loaded question
But the answer is an easy dream
To detect fire you must have fire
To detect passion you must have passion
Sense no burn and it is you who's numb
Taste no spice and it is you who's bland
There's nothing but the mirror and the window
All you see in this world is what you reflect
Until you see through the looking glass
Once you look within, you can look without
Unveiled eyes witness the grace of the soul
Earthly portals beyond the realm of illusion
Fire burns in the words you are reading now
Wild passion searing with conviction
My pen is ablaze with the ink-blood of my heart
These words are nothing before they are passion
A fury of fuel for an inner journey to my fiery core
My passion is the light in the night
Divine flames display this descent into my depths
And these words are an inferno

JRE
2011

This is the answer to a question that was once asked of me. At the time, my ego (my very childish ego) answered the question and gave a poor reply. I feel that I wrote this in a moment when my ego was checked and I was finally able to answer from my heart.

Story of My Life

I was born in the moon of the crimson calf with cowboys all around me
My rabbit came with me from last time I was here, but I preferred my teddy
I remember being bitten, but I can't recall if it was before or after my brother
Then, before I knew what was going on, the world changed and moved away
My new childhood was filled with reading buddies, doctor games, and fields of fire
I remember magic shows, fortune tellers, and that the lion slept one night
Then a wolverine came out of the dark, and nocturnal rage was unleashed upon the farm
Endless beginnings with never an ending, a thousand unfinished sagas lived in my mind
But soon I found myself wandering off the beaten path and lost among the leaves
A stranger appeared, a friend to me, an enemy to the rest, and he offered to save me
He set me on a cloud and sent me to the most colourful lights and the loudest sounds
I was buzzing when he gave me the crown I'd always wanted and told me I could have it all
But his living became the bad dose, and his dusk till dawn dance simply had to end
So it came to pass, I fell into the arms of an angel, and a cowboy put me back on the path
I was shown the love of our lives and actually had the Girl in my arms once or twice
But any man would deny his true path when not truly walking it, so I walked the lie
I inherited my ticket and I left the shelter of my life, well, left in body at least
The wolverine threw another smashing party, only this time a scandal was thrown in
But life changed again when a man from the west died and I came to life in a forest
I mounted a streamlined razorback and rode it back to where I started all this nonsense
In my new old home I found a nest of spiders with legs pointing in all different directions
But it was the Light shining on my real path that invited me to go back and walk the truth
So I did, and I walked far away from where the lie happened, and I found a cave
In the cave was a bear, and in the bear was my dream, and in the dream was the story of my lives
And so it was in the east that I stared into the eyes of the one responsible for all my trouble
We came to an understanding, an acceptance of how things are, and life went on
I found a whale inside me who started telling me secrets. I met a lizard who sees the future
I traded a new drum for a wise drum, or perhaps it was the other way around
Then, as I was solving people's problems the world over, a unicorn entered this fairy tale
It liked me so much that I did the only illogical thing to do; I hunted it
But the predator became the prey, and life became the deer's eyes and the hawk's call
I put on a new hat and stepped into the boots that are made for my trail in life
And everything that ended begins again with a thank you and a journey to the heart
JRE
2011

Literally the story of my life, just in need of a special limited edition JRE decoder ring.

Happily Ever After

It's after being taken away by everything in her eyes
It's after forgetting a person who'd taken so long to know
It's after giving into the wish of a woman with the softest hands
Broken thoughts in a broken mind, bloody feelings in a bleeding heart
Did you know there's a woman wandering around inside?
The footsteps of so many invitations trample over what took years to grow
I fell so hard for you, and where I fell from doesn't seem to matter anymore
In this place I can only shake the nonsense from my head
In this place I can only purge the emotion from my heart
My days are a pathetic plea for you to leave this body
My time is some bizarre hope to have you banished
But what a fool am I for the choice I'd make
To take you back when you've already been left behind
The sun sets on us and rises on the rest of our lives
I go back to the waterfall and the rain
With just that one memory plucked from all our time
That's how I would ask to keep you

JRE
2011

A piece inspired from the residual sentiments of a recent breakup. It's another story of two people who could have been so much more, if only they hadn't forgotten who they were. You often hear people say that it takes time for "true colours" to come out, and to make decisions based on those impressions. Sometimes I wonder if first impressions, while not everlasting, might be the best way to see who a person really hopes to be in life. After all, people can try not to change, but most times they can't help but grow.

The Devil's Fairy Tail

There's a fallen face that haunts this world
Behind a wide grin of alluring gold is where it hides
A cloak of ruby shade covers his crooked mouth
His creepy fingers reach passed his teeth and tongue
A long thread of silken promise unspools from his throat
He sees you wandering in and out of the sun
Casts the long line into the dark places of life
Luring with the easy deliverance of dreams and desires
His barbed hook snares you when you dive and hit bottom
Patient twirls reel you in from the end of the line
And, oh, the craftiest craft, the sneakiest sneak, the trickiest trick
He sells you he saved you
You feel ever so good as this spider spins
He offers to paint your life a masterpiece of poisonous pleasure
And your stupid smile watches you nod with eager enthusiasm
But you're too happy to see that he only stands in the shadows
Too thrilled to notice he only accommodates the choices he chooses
You're just too consumed to glimpse the way in which he abides
And when he crashes you all to pieces, you blame someone else
Crawl back to his insidious trap and plead for another dose
This clever lie is camouflaged as conscious, disguised as deliverance
But behind his mask are red eyes buried in tall, arched hallways of hell
Only he wields the power to break the rules that goodness lays and obeys
That's why you're lost in what he's found
You're just another shadow now
Just another bit of darkness to help him highlight the beacons
The candles that light his night, those are what he seeks to extinguish
The brighter the beam, the more tantalizing the target
His story is blurred and mostly forgotten, but he's always been there
He's got nothing left but to keep on with his ancient, withered agenda
Such a wretched and pathetic face that was once so beautiful
Thank him when he comes, and love him when he lies
After all, he was lost before you were

JRE
2011

A Warm Place

A summer day is always my greatest way, a long walk into the warmest place
Above me is the brilliance hanging like a blue curtain, the shroud that forever shelters
I thrive beneath this holy sky and think on the inside of my very own rainbow
Cotton clouds streak horizons with a masterful brush stroke, this is never before and never again
The sunset is an epic symphony of colourful hope, and I am surrounded by the high pitched chorus
Green on the grass so fair, leaves on emperor trees, so many birds have songs to sing
To take it in entirely and leave nothing on the outside would be a crime
But I am addicted to the whimsical world around me, and I suckle in bursts and spurts
Drenched in the sanctified life that is breathed in through the fantasy skin
My mind thinks on a hard morning of crispy white to highlight the careful balance
Our world is not what our eyes see now, but what exists when we're not looking
The mortal illusion that holds those who delve so far beyond ancient childhood
Smothered against the throbbing bosom of what we already decided to see
We grant ourselves rundown reasons in this, the beautiful season
And what was long forgotten has become a burden the few must carry for the many
This passion burns, but perhaps only for me, another will have to burn for you
Would you rather steal these words that would have been given to you?
The heavy curtain sky dangles night over these somber heads, the stars spin
A moonlight mirror on the soft, still water captures our deepest secret
Mingled in all our vain reflections is more than the desire to be forgiven
It is the almighty, hushed wish to have never done what needs the forgiving
We are bleeding out from this corroded wish and our life's time is what does the cutting
But laughter is the answer to this omnipotent prayer, real glee staring at our ugly face
We're just so happy to see ourselves here, and we'd be ever so delighted to stay
Better that the magical world is a stranger to us, the unreal unrealized in reality
Truth would be a long sacrificial slice in the tapestry of our blessed construct
Winter hearts feel no shame and only thaw at a touch from the holy gold
Sweet beautiful silence is the song sung in the hall of the mountain king
But from the deep caverns of the earth a voice rises and pounds on the stone door
Proclaiming the greatest story ever untold and something so important that most will not listen
And just to make its message clear, this story will only be carved in the dirt
The earth and the sky shall reclaim all they have given with an easy choice
Our time is imbued with the long silver light, and its sun makes all this a warm place

JRE
2011

This was reworked from a 2008 piece. The title has dual meaning, one of which is homage to Trent Reznor, whose 2010 work was used as an inspiration. Another personal favourite.

In the Shade of a Bleeding Heart

A Shadow is the finest mirror, for only it can show us all the same
Our lonely vanity leaves no trace when form is defined by light

Our red blood is proof of kin, even though it flows beneath our preferred masks
In our veins runs the thick crimson river that connects us to our common mother

In every heart resounds the pounding pulse that is our unified chorus
No angel on earth or heaven hears words before our sacred rhythm

In the shade of a bleeding heart we find our family
Truth, as it so often does, resides underneath the surface
But human eyes see the facade first, our deluded division
Seeping from our very skin is this maniacal manifestation
We stare at difference like a beacon in the blackest night
Choosing to stand alone in the dark and cut out our bleeding hearts
Who notices the pumping puddle of life lurking in the shadows?
To nourish and love your own tree, but chop down another's...
To start or finish are always the reasons we cough up
But a severed limb from the tree of life is everyone's wound
One less shadow
One less river
One less heart
One less life
Divide even the largest sum enough times and eventually you reach zero

JRE
2011

This was nursed from a piece written in 2008. It's about the human tendency to notice the few differences between us and ignore our more vast and important similarities.

Tomorrow

Winds of hope to carry this perfect passion
Unfurled in the world's light, the reminiscence
Touch the memory of man with songs of empty grave
When the dim echo ascends the volume is idea and reason
Pointing to the destined connection of bold action and purpose

Black hands recoil with attempts to leave the tainted touch
A forceful ugly scar reflected in all we do
The stolen sun does return and finds resolve true
New life and careful dawn, the motion of this mind
Red blood memory released with the divine essence

Forgotten, rotting, challenged and tried in death, slain by our flight
Look to the twilit skies when sunset words define this fate pure
Soft feather dream caught in a breeze of compelling innocence
Rise in the night to wish for our triumphant morning
When stars are our friends and born is the locked promise

To own the day we gave away, the bane of our curious heart
Shackles cracked and lies revealed in our patient birth
Washed and bathed in the sweetest place
Watched and embraced by our favourite face
Where the heart is enriched with the company of compassion

The dawn is come redeeming the complacent past
Swallowed demon thoughts now digested and expelled
Revive the sanctified spirit of yesterdays forgot and tomorrows never known
Alive in realized surprise before all our waking eyes
And in the morning a silver sunrise that dries all tears cried

JRE
2007

> Written on Christmas Day 2007, this has dual meaning. One meaning relates these words to a relationship that was beginning under unusual circumstances. The other is a greater meaning that I see applying to everyone, leaving no person unaffected. This piece is another favourite and, in my view, the perfect ending.

About the Poet

Jeffrey began writing poetry in 1998 and has always found personal freedom with his expressive pen. He was born in 1981, the eldest son to *Ron* and *Diane Erdman*. He has one brother, *Gregory*, born 1983. Originally from Ontario, Canada, *Jeffrey* moved to Nova Scotia in 2009.

Besides writing poetry and fiction, his passion lies in the especially unique style of Reiki Energy Healing that is offered exclusively through *Journey to the Heart*, located in Tatamagouche, Nova Scotia. *Jeffrey* has been a "patient" and "student" of this particular brand of Reiki for almost 10 years. He enjoys representing *Journey to the Heart* as an advocate and associate at promotional events for this distinctive form of Reiki.

He enjoys the company of his cats, *Pacha* (Incan for Cosmic Mother), and *Coto* (Incan for A Handful of Seeds, or the Pleiades). *Jeffrey's* favourite book is *The Celestine Prophecy* (and series), written by *James Redfield*. His favourite film is *Avatar*, directed by his all-time favourite director, *James Cameron*. Close seconds are *Dances With Wolves*, *Apocalypto*, and *Legends of the Fall*.

Jeffrey is an avid music lover whose tastes are eclectic and vast. His favourite genres include (good) Country, Classic Rock, 80's Retro, New Age, Trance/Progressive, Classical, and so much more. He spent a few years in his youth learning electric guitar, but gave it up in 2000 in favour of 2 turntables and a mixing board (Technics 1200's and a Pioneer DJM 909). He gigged in Ontario for several years under the DJ name *Chuck Li*, however, although he still has much passion, he gave up the DJ life in 2009. His favourite DJ is *Eddie Halliwell*.

Jeffrey enjoys his easy-breezy life in Nova Scotia, and gives every effort to seeing as many sunsets as is humanly possible.

Coming Soon...

~ Footprints On the Water ~

A work of fiction from Jeffrey R. Erdman

www.ingramcontent.com/pod-product-compliance
Lightning Source LLC
LaVergne TN
LVHW051509070426
835507LV00022B/3015